Regenerative Agriculture: A Global Climate Solutions Insight on Building Soil Health, Reducing Emissions, Improving Resilience, and Restoring Ecosystems

I0116198

1

Copyright

Regenerative Agriculture: A Global Climate Solutions Insight on Building Soil Health, Reducing Emissions, Improving Resilience, and Restoring Ecosystems

ISBN (eBook): 978-1-991368-03-4

ISBN (Paperback): 978-1-991368-04-1

Published by Global Climate Solutions

First Edition, 2025

Cover design and interior layout by Global Climate Solutions

Table of Contents

Introduction

Regenerative agriculture is a holistic farming approach that places soil health, biodiversity, and ecosystem services at the center of food production, while also acting as a powerful tool for carbon sequestration and climate resilience. Unlike conventional sustainability strategies that focus on minimizing harm, regenerative practices seek to restore natural systems, offering a pathway to rebuild degraded soils, enhance water cycles, and support thriving rural communities. As agriculture is responsible for a significant proportion of global greenhouse gas emissions and land degradation, transitioning to regenerative systems is increasingly recognized as essential for meeting climate targets, safeguarding food security, and protecting natural resources.

This Insight examines the core pillars required to mainstream regenerative agriculture: supportive policy frameworks, innovative financial mechanisms, and emerging technologies. By identifying practical solutions for decision-makers, it provides a roadmap for embedding regenerative agriculture across a range of contexts, from small-scale farms to large agribusiness. The focus is on fostering policy coherence, unlocking investment, and leveraging digital innovation to accelerate the adoption of regenerative practices. Through this lens, regenerative agriculture emerges not only as an environmental imperative but as a strategic foundation for sustainable, climate-resilient food systems and equitable rural development.

Chapter 1: Policy Frameworks for Scaling Regenerative Agriculture

Effective policy frameworks are essential for mainstreaming regenerative agriculture and driving large-scale transformation across food systems. By aligning national climate commitments, land-use regulations, and rural development strategies, governments can create the enabling conditions needed to support soil restoration, biodiversity, and climate resilience. This chapter explores the policy levers—ranging from integrated climate action plans and subsidy reforms to inclusive governance structures—that empower decision-makers to accelerate the adoption and scaling of regenerative practices in diverse agricultural landscapes.

1.1 Aligning Regenerative Agriculture with Climate and Land-Use Policies

Aligning regenerative agriculture with climate and land-use policies is essential for unlocking its full potential as a driver of climate mitigation, adaptation, and rural transformation. As countries update their Nationally Determined Contributions (NDCs) under the Paris Agreement, there is a growing opportunity to embed regenerative approaches as key strategies for delivering emission reductions and building climate resilience in the agricultural sector.

Positioning Regenerative Agriculture within Nationally Determined Contributions (NDCs):

NDCs set the framework for national climate action, and agriculture is central to many countries' commitments. By explicitly recognizing regenerative agriculture as a pathway to achieve mitigation and adaptation targets, governments can elevate the importance of practices such as cover cropping, agroforestry, rotational grazing, and integrated crop-livestock systems. Inclusion in NDCs signals political commitment, unlocks technical and financial support, and encourages coordination across ministries.

Countries leading in this area are developing measurable targets for soil carbon sequestration, improved biodiversity, and reduced agricultural emissions as part of their climate strategies, providing a model for integrating regenerative outcomes into future NDCs.

Integration into Land Restoration, Biodiversity, and Soil Health Policies:

Regenerative agriculture is uniquely positioned at the intersection of land restoration, biodiversity protection, and soil health improvement. Policies such as national land degradation neutrality strategies, biodiversity action plans, and soil health initiatives can be aligned with regenerative principles to create synergies across sectors. This includes incentivizing practices that rebuild organic matter, enhance pollinator habitats, and restore degraded landscapes. Coherent integration reduces duplication, maximizes impact, and ensures that efforts in one policy arena reinforce gains in others. For example, connecting regenerative practices to national soil health policies can mobilize public funding, research, and extension services toward widespread adoption.

Policy Coherence Across Agriculture, Forestry, Water, and Climate Sectors:

Achieving policy coherence is critical for scaling regenerative agriculture beyond niche applications. Fragmented governance—where agriculture, forestry, water, and climate policies operate in silos—can undermine the effectiveness of regenerative interventions. Integrated policy frameworks that align objectives, incentives, and monitoring systems across these sectors enable more efficient resource use, reduce conflicting land-use pressures, and support multifunctional landscapes. This approach strengthens the resilience of food systems and rural economies to climate shocks and environmental risks. Effective cross-sectoral coordination can be achieved through joint task forces, integrated land-use plans, and inter-ministerial committees focused on holistic, landscape-level solutions.

By embedding regenerative agriculture within climate and land-use policies, countries can drive systemic change that supports climate goals, ecosystem restoration, and sustainable livelihoods. This alignment ensures that regenerative approaches move from the margins to the mainstream of national development and climate strategies.

1.2 Designing Supportive Legal and Regulatory Instruments

Supportive legal and regulatory instruments are foundational for enabling the transition to regenerative agriculture at scale. Robust frameworks create the right incentives, remove barriers, and provide security for farmers and land managers adopting regenerative practices. They ensure that policy intent translates into meaningful, long-term action on the ground.

Reforming Subsidies to Incentivize Ecosystem Restoration:

Traditional agricultural subsidies have often favored high-input, intensive production models that can drive land degradation and biodiversity loss. To support regenerative agriculture, subsidies must be redirected toward ecosystem restoration and soil-building practices. This involves shifting financial incentives to reward outcomes such as increased soil organic matter, water retention, and habitat restoration. Performance-based payments and environmental stewardship schemes can encourage farmers to adopt regenerative techniques, fostering a transition away from extractive models. Clear eligibility criteria, transparent reporting, and regular evaluation ensure that subsidies drive measurable ecosystem improvements.

Establishing Land Tenure and Carbon Rights for Regenerative Practices:

Secure land tenure is essential for encouraging long-term investments in soil health, reforestation, and other regenerative actions. Legal recognition of tenure rights—including for smallholders, indigenous peoples, and local communities— empowers land stewards to invest in restorative practices with confidence. In parallel, establishing clear and enforceable carbon rights allows farmers to participate in carbon markets and benefit financially from sequestration activities. Transparent carbon accounting, verification systems, and legal frameworks are necessary to ensure that carbon benefits are attributed fairly, reducing the risk of land grabs and ensuring social equity in regenerative transitions.

Regulatory Frameworks for Biodiversity-Enhancing Land Use:

Regulatory approaches play a key role in safeguarding and enhancing biodiversity within agricultural landscapes. This includes developing and enforcing standards for buffer zones, wildlife corridors, and pollinator habitats on farmland. Regulations can require the preservation or restoration of native vegetation, support mixed cropping and agroforestry, and protect high-value conservation areas. Effective enforcement, monitoring, and compliance mechanisms are necessary to ensure that legal requirements drive genuine landscape regeneration. Complementary measures—such as technical assistance and market access for biodiversity-friendly products—can support compliance and promote uptake of biodiversity-enhancing practices.

A strong legal and regulatory foundation is a critical lever for mainstreaming regenerative agriculture, ensuring that financial incentives, property rights, and land-use requirements work in concert to accelerate ecosystem restoration, climate action, and rural prosperity.

1.3 Institutional Capacity and Multi-Level Governance

Building institutional capacity and fostering multi-level governance are essential for scaling regenerative agriculture from pilot projects to widespread practice. Effective institutions empower farmers, coordinate across administrative levels, and support learning and adaptation, ensuring that regenerative approaches are integrated into everyday land management decisions.

Strengthening Extension Services with Regenerative Knowledge:

Extension services are vital conduits for delivering technical support and knowledge to farmers. Strengthening these services with expertise in regenerative practices—such as soil health management, cover cropping, agroforestry, and rotational grazing—enables broader adoption of climate-resilient methods. Training extension officers, developing region-specific resources, and embedding regenerative principles into curricula increase the capacity to deliver tailored, actionable advice. Collaborative partnerships with research institutions, NGOs, and farmer organizations further enhance the reach and effectiveness of extension systems, facilitating peer learning and innovation diffusion.

Role of Local and Regional Governments in Land-Use Planning:

Local and regional governments are on the front lines of land-use planning and resource management. Their ability to integrate regenerative agriculture into zoning laws, land-use plans, and rural development strategies can catalyze large-scale transitions. These authorities can implement incentives for regenerative land management, support demonstration sites, and coordinate across sectors such as agriculture, forestry, and water management. By embedding regenerative goals in local policies and budgets, subnational governments play a direct role in scaling practices and mobilizing local action aligned with national and global climate targets.

Enhancing Participatory Governance with Indigenous and Farmer Networks:

Inclusive and participatory governance is crucial for ensuring that regenerative agriculture is context-appropriate and socially equitable. Indigenous peoples and local farming communities hold valuable traditional knowledge and have a direct stake in land management outcomes. Institutionalizing participatory processes—such as community consultations, co-management frameworks, and farmer-led councils—strengthens decision-making, fosters local ownership, and ensures that diverse perspectives shape policy and implementation. Supporting the formation and operation of farmer and indigenous networks also builds social capital, facilitates exchange of best practices, and enables advocacy for regenerative approaches at all levels of governance.

A robust governance structure that connects institutions from national to local levels, strengthens extension systems, and embraces participatory models is critical for embedding regenerative agriculture within rural landscapes. Such arrangements create an enabling environment for innovation, learning, and resilience—paving the way for long-term, landscape-scale transformation.

1.4 National and Regional Policy Instruments

National and regional policy instruments play a central role in translating high-level commitments on regenerative agriculture into actionable measures that drive change across landscapes and markets. Well-crafted instruments provide direction, set standards, and create incentives that guide the actions of farmers, agribusinesses, and public agencies.

Agroecology Action Plans and Soil Health Roadmaps:

Governments are increasingly adopting agroecology action plans and soil health roadmaps to provide a structured pathway for advancing regenerative agriculture. These plans typically outline targets for improving soil organic matter, restoring degraded land, and scaling agroecological practices. They identify priority interventions, allocate resources for research and extension, and establish monitoring frameworks to track progress. By linking these roadmaps to broader sustainable development objectives, governments ensure that regenerative agriculture contributes to climate resilience, biodiversity, and rural livelihoods at scale.

Public Procurement and Supply Chain Standards Promoting Regenerative Outputs:

Public procurement policies are powerful tools for stimulating demand for regenerative agricultural products. By setting sustainability criteria and favoring regenerative outputs—such as crops grown with soil-building practices or livestock raised under holistic grazing—governments can create stable markets and incentivize adoption. Similarly, developing supply chain standards that prioritize transparency, traceability, and ecosystem benefits drives private sector alignment. Certification schemes, labeling, and preferential purchasing programs not only reward regenerative producers but also encourage large agribusinesses and retailers to integrate these principles into their sourcing strategies.

Integration into National Adaptation Plans and Food Security Strategies:

Mainstreaming regenerative agriculture into national adaptation plans (NAPs) and food security strategies strengthens the resilience of food systems to climate change and other shocks. Incorporating regenerative practices into NAPs enables governments to leverage climate finance, coordinate sectoral adaptation efforts, and build the capacity of farming communities to respond to climate risks. Aligning food security policies with regenerative approaches supports sustainable intensification, reduces vulnerability to supply disruptions, and enhances nutritional outcomes. Coordinated policy integration ensures that regenerative agriculture is embedded within the country's long-term vision for food systems and rural development.

Collectively, these national and regional instruments provide a comprehensive policy architecture that supports the transition toward regenerative agriculture, linking on-the-ground action with strategic goals for climate resilience, ecosystem restoration, and sustainable rural economies.

1.5 International Cooperation and Global Agreements

International cooperation and alignment with global agreements are essential for scaling regenerative agriculture and embedding it in the world's climate and sustainability agenda. Collaborative action across borders fosters knowledge exchange, resource mobilization, and the development of consistent standards that accelerate regenerative transitions worldwide.

Mainstreaming Regenerative Agriculture in UNFCCC, CBD, and UNCCD Frameworks:

Integrating regenerative agriculture into major international frameworks—including the United Nations Framework Convention on Climate Change (UNFCCC), the Convention on Biological Diversity (CBD), and the United Nations Convention to Combat Desertification (UNCCD)—ensures that regenerative principles are reflected in global policy, finance, and reporting mechanisms. This mainstreaming strengthens the link between agricultural transformation and climate, biodiversity, and land restoration goals. By embedding regenerative outcomes in Nationally Determined Contributions, biodiversity targets, and land degradation neutrality strategies, countries can access technical support, climate finance, and international cooperation channels dedicated to advancing regenerative systems.

Promoting South-South and North-South Collaboration on Technical and Policy Transfer:

Effective diffusion of regenerative agriculture depends on robust knowledge exchange and technical assistance between countries. South-South collaboration enables developing countries with similar agro-ecological contexts to share practical solutions, co-develop technologies, and build capacity for implementation. North-South partnerships facilitate the transfer of research, finance, and policy innovations, ensuring that best practices and cutting-edge tools are adapted and adopted in diverse settings. International platforms, twinning arrangements, and joint pilot projects accelerate the scaling of regenerative agriculture by leveraging collective expertise and experience across regions.

Role of Multilateral Institutions in Harmonizing Global Regenerative Targets:

Multilateral organizations—including the Food and Agriculture Organization (FAO), the World Bank, and regional development banks—play a critical role in coordinating global action on regenerative agriculture. By developing harmonized definitions, monitoring frameworks, and investment guidelines, these institutions provide clarity and consistency that drive greater alignment among countries and stakeholders. They also serve as conveners for global dialogues, mobilize resources for regenerative initiatives, and support the creation of shared metrics for measuring progress. Through technical assistance, policy advocacy, and funding, multilateral bodies help ensure that regenerative agriculture becomes a central pillar of global climate and development agendas.

International cooperation anchored in strong global agreements and multilateral action is key to realizing the full potential of regenerative agriculture. By working together, countries can create an enabling environment for transformative change—ensuring that regenerative systems deliver climate, biodiversity, and development benefits at scale.

Chapter 2: Financial Mechanisms and Incentives for Transition

Unlocking the full potential of regenerative agriculture depends on the availability of targeted financial mechanisms and incentives that support farmers and businesses throughout the transition. Redirecting agricultural finance, innovating payment systems, and mobilizing climate investment are essential to overcome barriers and catalyze large-scale change. This chapter examines how public and private capital, climate funds, and impact investment tools can be harnessed to create rewarding, resilient, and equitable financial environments for scaling regenerative agriculture.

2.1 Redirecting Agricultural Finance Toward Regenerative Outcomes

Redirecting agricultural finance toward regenerative outcomes is a pivotal step in catalyzing the shift from conventional practices to systems that build soil health, enhance biodiversity, and improve climate resilience. Targeted financial instruments and investment frameworks can unlock widespread adoption by making regenerative agriculture more accessible and attractive to farmers and agribusinesses.

Reforming Agricultural Credit and Insurance to Favor Soil-Enhancing Practices:

Traditional credit and insurance products often reinforce input-intensive farming and offer limited incentives for adopting regenerative approaches. Reform is needed to ensure financial services recognize the long-term benefits and risk reductions provided by regenerative practices. Credit schemes can be adapted to offer preferential rates or terms for farmers who implement cover cropping, agroforestry, reduced tillage, and other soil-enhancing methods. Similarly, insurance products should factor in the resilience gains from regenerative systems, such as improved drought tolerance and lower susceptibility to pest outbreaks, thus lowering premiums for regenerative producers. This creates a powerful incentive for transition while reducing systemic risks in the agricultural sector.

De-risking Investments Through Blended Finance and Guarantee Mechanisms:

Investing in regenerative agriculture can be perceived as risky, especially for early adopters and smallholders. Blended finance— combining public, philanthropic, and private capital—can de-risk investments and encourage greater participation from commercial banks and investors. Guarantee mechanisms, such as first-loss capital or risk-sharing facilities, further reduce financial exposure for lenders and investors, making it more viable to finance regenerative projects at scale. These approaches mobilize resources for infrastructure, technology, and working capital, accelerating the adoption of regenerative practices across diverse farming systems.

Public-Private Partnerships to Support Climate-Smart Value Chains:

Effective collaboration between the public and private sectors is essential for developing climate-smart value chains that reward regenerative producers. Governments can provide enabling policies, co-investment, and market development support, while private companies contribute technical expertise, market access, and value-added services. Such partnerships can create integrated supply chains that incentivize regenerative production, from input provision and farm support to processing, certification, and market linkage. By aligning public investment with private sector innovation, these partnerships drive economies of scale, attract investment, and help build resilient, inclusive agricultural markets that prioritize regenerative outcomes.

Redirecting finance in these ways is fundamental to transforming agricultural systems, ensuring that capital flows support practices and business models that contribute to long-term environmental health, food security, and climate stability.

2.2 Payment for Ecosystem Services (PES) and Carbon Markets

PES and carbon markets offer critical financial incentives for adopting regenerative agriculture by directly rewarding the delivery of ecosystem benefits. These mechanisms can drive landscape-scale transformation by recognizing and monetizing the positive externalities generated by regenerative practices, including carbon sequestration, improved water cycles, and enhanced biodiversity.

Structuring PES Schemes Around Soil Carbon, Water Retention, and Biodiversity:

Effective PES schemes identify, quantify, and value the ecosystem services provided by regenerative agriculture. This often involves creating metrics and baselines for soil carbon storage, water retention, and biodiversity indicators such as habitat quality or pollinator abundance. By establishing clear criteria and performance benchmarks, PES programs can channel payments to farmers and land managers who deliver verified improvements in these areas. Payment levels should reflect the value of ecosystem services to society and incentivize continuous improvement. Transparent monitoring, reporting, and verification systems ensure that payments are based on real, measurable outcomes, increasing trust and participation.

Integrating Regenerative Practices Into Voluntary and Compliance Carbon Markets:

Regenerative agriculture has significant potential to contribute to both voluntary and compliance carbon markets through increased soil carbon sequestration and reduced greenhouse gas emissions. Integrating regenerative practices into existing market frameworks requires robust methodologies for quantifying, verifying, and certifying soil carbon gains and other emission reductions. Projects can generate carbon credits that are sold to companies and governments seeking to offset emissions, creating a new revenue stream for farmers. Alignment with recognized standards and registries enhances the credibility and market value of regenerative carbon credits, supporting the scalability and impact of these initiatives.

Ensuring Equity and Transparency in Benefit-Sharing Mechanisms:

For PES and carbon markets to deliver lasting benefits, equity and transparency must be embedded in their design and implementation. Clear rules for participation, accessible information, and fair distribution of payments are essential to ensure smallholders, women, indigenous peoples, and marginalized groups are not excluded. Benefit-sharing arrangements should recognize customary rights and ensure that communities actively participating in regenerative land management receive a fair share of rewards. Independent oversight, stakeholder engagement, and regular evaluation strengthen transparency, accountability, and social legitimacy, helping PES and carbon market initiatives build trust and deliver inclusive development outcomes.

Together, PES and carbon markets offer powerful levers for scaling regenerative agriculture, turning ecosystem stewardship into a viable and attractive livelihood strategy while supporting global climate and biodiversity goals.

2.3 Climate Funds and Green Bonds

Mobilizing climate funds and green bonds is central to accelerating investment in regenerative agriculture and land-based climate solutions. These financial instruments channel resources into projects that deliver measurable environmental, social, and economic benefits, supporting a large-scale transition toward resilient and sustainable food systems.

Leveraging the Green Climate Fund and Adaptation Fund for Land-Based Solutions:

The Green Climate Fund (GCF) and Adaptation Fund are among the world's largest climate finance vehicles, designed to support developing countries in achieving their climate mitigation and adaptation goals. By positioning regenerative agriculture as a key solution within project proposals, governments and implementing agencies can secure funding for activities such as soil restoration, water conservation, agroforestry, and climate-smart land management. Accessing these funds typically requires robust project design, clear environmental and social safeguards, and transparent monitoring and reporting frameworks. Successful projects often demonstrate how regenerative approaches contribute to both emission reductions and enhanced climate resilience, making them highly competitive in the climate finance landscape.

Designing Regenerative Agriculture Bonds and Impact Investment Tools:

Green bonds and impact investment vehicles tailored to regenerative agriculture enable both public and private sector investors to support projects with clear sustainability outcomes. Regenerative agriculture bonds can finance activities ranging from the adoption of soil health practices and ecosystem restoration to farm-scale infrastructure and community-based projects. Impact investors seek measurable environmental and social returns alongside financial performance, making rigorous selection criteria and transparent reporting essential. Certification by recognized standards, such as the Climate Bonds Initiative, enhances credibility and attracts a wider pool of investors, while innovative structures—such as blended finance and outcome-based payments—can further scale up investment flows.

Linking Climate Finance to Food System Transformation Strategies:

Integrating regenerative agriculture into broader food system transformation strategies ensures that climate finance delivers both environmental impact and systemic change. This involves aligning investments with national food security and rural development policies, building multi-stakeholder coalitions, and fostering cross-sectoral coordination. Climate finance mechanisms can be structured to support the scaling of regenerative supply chains, value-added processing, and market development for regenerative products. Embedding regenerative agriculture in food system strategies leverages the full potential of climate funds and green bonds to drive innovation, build resilience, and achieve lasting transformation across landscapes.

By harnessing climate funds and green bonds, stakeholders can unlock new sources of capital for regenerative agriculture, ensuring that the financial sector becomes a key ally in building sustainable, climate-resilient food systems worldwide.

2.4 Philanthropic and Multilateral Grantmaking

Philanthropic and multilateral grantmaking plays a pivotal role in advancing regenerative agriculture, especially in regions and communities that may lack access to commercial finance or public investment. By strategically directing resources, these grants can catalyze innovation, build capacity, and support inclusive transitions toward regenerative systems at scale.

Aligning Philanthropic Funding with Place-Based Regenerative Priorities:

Effective philanthropic investment begins with a deep understanding of local agro-ecological, social, and economic contexts. By aligning funding priorities with the unique needs of regions and communities, philanthropic organizations can drive targeted support for locally relevant regenerative practices. This might include supporting indigenous land management, community-led restoration projects, or the introduction of regenerative methods adapted to local crops and landscapes. Flexible grant structures, long-term commitments, and participatory grantmaking processes empower communities to shape priorities and solutions, ensuring that interventions are context-appropriate and sustainable.

Facilitating Donor Alignment Around Global Soil Health Targets:

Global challenges—such as soil degradation and loss of soil organic matter—require coordinated action across multiple donors and stakeholders. Philanthropic foundations, bilateral agencies, and multilateral organizations can enhance impact by aligning around common goals and targets, such as those established by the United Nations or regional soil health initiatives. Donor platforms, pooled funds, and joint investment strategies can increase the scale and coherence of funding, reduce duplication, and facilitate knowledge exchange. This collaborative approach strengthens efforts to achieve widespread improvements in soil health, biodiversity, and carbon sequestration through regenerative agriculture.

Enhancing Grant-Based Support for Smallholder-Led Transition Pathways:

Smallholder farmers are central to the global food system and are often at the forefront of both vulnerability and opportunity in regenerative transitions. Grants targeted at smallholder-led initiatives can support access to training, inputs, technology, and markets needed to implement regenerative practices. Capacity-building programs, demonstration sites, and farmer-to-farmer knowledge exchange networks help accelerate adoption and adaptation. Furthermore, grants that prioritize social inclusion—such as those supporting women, youth, and indigenous farmers—promote equitable outcomes and ensure that the benefits of regenerative agriculture are widely shared.

By leveraging philanthropic and multilateral grants, stakeholders can address funding gaps, foster innovation, and build inclusive pathways for the large-scale adoption of regenerative agriculture, ultimately strengthening the resilience and sustainability of food systems around the world.

2.5 Monitoring, Reporting, and Verification (MRV) for Financial Instruments

MRV systems are fundamental for ensuring that financial instruments supporting regenerative agriculture deliver real, measurable, and transparent outcomes. Effective MRV frameworks build trust among funders, implementers, and beneficiaries, while enabling continuous improvement and accountability in regenerative initiatives.

Designing Robust MRV Systems for Regenerative Outcomes:

A well-designed MRV system captures data on the key environmental, social, and economic impacts of regenerative agriculture. This includes quantifying changes in soil organic carbon, biodiversity, water retention, and farm productivity, as well as social metrics such as livelihoods and gender inclusion. MRV methodologies must be scientifically rigorous, context-specific, and cost-effective to implement at scale. Advances in digital technology—such as remote sensing, mobile data collection, and geospatial analytics—facilitate accurate and timely tracking of outcomes. Involving farmers and local stakeholders in data gathering strengthens accuracy and ownership while ensuring the system reflects ground realities.

Linking MRV to Access and Disbursement of Funds:

Linking MRV results to the flow of financial resources increases the effectiveness and impact of funding mechanisms. Disbursement of grants, loans, or incentive payments can be tied to the achievement of verified regenerative outcomes, ensuring that resources reward genuine improvements rather than intentions alone. Performance-based financing encourages continual progress, supports transparency, and reduces the risk of misallocation. Clear reporting requirements and independent verification build credibility, attract investment, and enable adaptive management in response to observed results.

Harmonizing Indicators Across Ecosystems, Soil Health, and Carbon Accounting:

Consistency in indicators and methodologies is critical for aggregating results across projects, regions, and funding streams. Harmonizing metrics for soil health, ecosystem restoration, biodiversity, and carbon sequestration enables comparison, learning, and scaling of best practices. Alignment with recognized standards—such as those developed by international organizations, carbon registries, or sustainability frameworks—facilitates interoperability and streamlines reporting for stakeholders participating in multiple programs. Standardized approaches also support the creation of credible, high-integrity markets for ecosystem services and carbon credits linked to regenerative agriculture.

By establishing strong MRV systems, financial instruments can reliably channel capital to projects that deliver proven regenerative benefits, advancing the credibility, impact, and scalability of the regenerative agriculture movement.

Chapter 3: Technology and Innovation for Regenerative Systems

Technology and innovation are driving forces behind the widespread adoption of regenerative agriculture. Digital tools, biological inputs, precision equipment, and collaborative innovation platforms are transforming how farmers restore soil health, enhance biodiversity, and increase climate resilience. This chapter explores the latest advancements empowering regenerative systems, from data-driven decision-making and nature-based solutions to open-source knowledge sharing and public-private partnerships, highlighting how innovation ecosystems accelerate the scaling and effectiveness of regenerative agriculture worldwide.

3.1 Digital Tools for Soil Health and Farm Management

Digital tools are revolutionizing the way regenerative agriculture is practiced, enabling farmers and land managers to make data-driven decisions that enhance soil health, optimize resource use, and build climate resilience. Advanced technologies are increasing the accuracy, speed, and scale at which regenerative practices can be adopted, monitored, and adapted.

GIS and Remote Sensing for Land-Use Diagnostics and Impact Tracking:

Geographic Information Systems (GIS) and remote sensing technologies provide powerful capabilities for mapping, diagnosing, and tracking changes in land use over time. Satellite imagery, drone surveys, and GIS platforms enable the identification of soil degradation, vegetation cover, water cycles, and biodiversity hotspots across landscapes. These tools allow stakeholders to assess baseline conditions, monitor the impacts of regenerative interventions, and identify areas needing targeted action. Regular analysis of remotely sensed data supports adaptive management by providing timely feedback on the effectiveness of regenerative practices at field, farm, and regional scales.

Mobile and IoT Platforms for Monitoring Soil Carbon and Nutrient Cycles:

Mobile applications and Internet of Things (IoT) sensors are making real-time monitoring of soil conditions accessible to farmers of all scales. IoT devices—such as soil probes and wireless sensors—measure key parameters including soil moisture, temperature, pH, and nutrient content, transmitting data directly to farm management systems or mobile devices. These insights support better decisions on irrigation, fertilization, and crop rotation, ensuring that regenerative practices are tailored to actual field conditions. Mobile platforms also facilitate knowledge sharing, data recording, and integration with digital advisory services, strengthening farmers' capacity to track progress and respond to changing environmental factors.

Decision-Support Systems for Climate-Resilient Regenerative Planning:

Sophisticated decision-support systems harness data analytics, artificial intelligence, and predictive modeling to guide regenerative management choices. These platforms synthesize information from diverse sources—including weather forecasts, soil health data, and crop performance—to recommend actions such as planting times, crop selection, and soil amendments. By accounting for local climate risks and ecological dynamics, decision-support tools help farmers implement practices that boost resilience, productivity, and environmental outcomes. Customizable interfaces and scenario planning features empower users to test different regenerative strategies and make informed, forward-looking decisions.

Collectively, these digital innovations are essential for mainstreaming regenerative agriculture, providing the tools needed to measure, manage, and maximize the benefits of healthy soils and resilient landscapes.

3.2 Innovations in Biological Inputs and Natural Amendments

Biological inputs and natural amendments are at the heart of regenerative agriculture, driving improvements in soil health, ecosystem function, and farm productivity. Innovations in this area are enabling farmers to restore natural cycles, reduce reliance on synthetic inputs, and foster resilience in both crops and soils.

Advances in Biofertilizers, Composts, and Microbial Treatments:

Cutting-edge biofertilizers leverage living microorganisms—such as nitrogen-fixing bacteria, mycorrhizal fungi, and phosphate-solubilizing microbes—to enhance nutrient availability and promote plant health. Composting innovations have improved the quality and efficiency of organic matter decomposition, yielding amendments rich in stable carbon and beneficial organisms. Microbial treatments, including soil inoculants and biostimulants, are being developed to boost soil fertility, suppress pathogens, and stimulate plant growth. These products not only reduce the need for chemical fertilizers but also improve soil structure, water retention, and the biological diversity necessary for resilient farming systems.

Seed Systems for Biodiversity and Crop Adaptation:

Innovative seed systems are facilitating access to diverse, locally adapted, and resilient crop varieties. Regenerative agriculture benefits from open-pollinated, heirloom, and regionally bred seeds that support biodiversity both on-farm and in surrounding ecosystems. Breeding programs now focus on traits such as drought tolerance, pest resistance, and nutritional quality, aligned with ecological principles rather than intensive input requirements. Seed exchanges, community seed banks, and participatory breeding empower farmers to maintain and develop genetic resources suited to their landscapes, bolstering both food security and ecosystem health.

Phasing Out Synthetic Inputs Through Innovation in Regenerative Input Markets:

The transition away from synthetic fertilizers and pesticides is being accelerated by the growth of regenerative input markets. New business models and products emphasize renewable, biologically based alternatives that align with soil health and environmental goals. This includes the development of organic amendments, natural pest deterrents, and mineral supplements derived from sustainable sources. Policy incentives, research investment, and certification schemes are supporting the market viability of these inputs, helping farmers overcome barriers to adoption. The result is a steadily expanding ecosystem of products and services that enable producers to maintain productivity and profitability while regenerating natural resources.

Ongoing innovation in biological inputs and natural amendments is fundamental to the success of regenerative agriculture, equipping farmers with tools that build soil vitality, reduce environmental impact, and sustain agricultural landscapes for future generations.

3.3 Mechanization and Precision Agriculture for Regeneration

Modern mechanization and precision agriculture are transforming the scalability and effectiveness of regenerative farming. By leveraging technology designed specifically for ecological restoration and resource efficiency, farmers can implement regenerative practices with greater accuracy, consistency, and impact across diverse landscapes.

Low-Disturbance and No-Till Technologies:

Conventional tillage often disrupts soil structure, depletes organic matter, and accelerates erosion. In contrast, low-disturbance and no-till equipment enables the establishment of crops with minimal soil disturbance, protecting soil health and fostering carbon sequestration. Innovations such as direct seeders, strip-till planters, and roller-crimpers allow farmers to manage cover crops and residue effectively while preserving microbial life and soil aggregates. Adoption of these technologies reduces labor and fuel use, lowers input costs, and enhances resilience to drought and flooding by improving soil structure and moisture retention.

Agroforestry and Silvopasture-Compatible Equipment:

Scaling agroforestry and silvopasture systems—where trees, crops, and livestock are integrated—requires specialized machinery that can operate in complex, multi-layered environments. Equipment such as narrow-profile tractors, mobile tree planters, and adaptable harvesting tools enable farmers to manage both woody and herbaceous components efficiently. Livestock management tools tailored for silvopasture support rotational grazing and facilitate the regeneration of understory vegetation. These advances help maximize the ecological benefits of integrated systems, including shade, habitat, and nutrient cycling, while supporting practical, profitable farm operations.

Precision Irrigation and Nutrient Delivery Systems to Restore Water Balance:

Water management is a cornerstone of regenerative agriculture. Precision irrigation technologies—such as drip systems, soil moisture sensors, and automated controllers—deliver water directly to plant roots, minimizing waste and reducing evaporation. Coupled with precision nutrient delivery, these systems ensure that crops receive optimal nutrition based on real-time soil and crop data, improving yields and reducing runoff and leaching. Smart irrigation and fertigation platforms can be integrated with weather data and remote sensing, enabling adaptive management that sustains soil health and conserves water resources, even under changing climate conditions.

By embracing mechanization and precision agriculture tailored for regeneration, farmers can scale up practices that build soil health, enhance biodiversity, and restore ecosystem functions—making regenerative agriculture both practical and high-performing for the future of food production.

3.4 Blockchain and Traceability Technologies

Blockchain and traceability technologies are unlocking new opportunities for transparency, accountability, and value creation in regenerative agriculture. By enabling secure, tamper-proof tracking of products and practices across the supply chain, these digital solutions help build trust among consumers, investors, and regulators, while rewarding farmers for sustainable outcomes.

Digital Ledgers for Regenerative Certification and Verification:

Blockchain-based digital ledgers provide an immutable record of regenerative practices—from soil management and crop inputs to biodiversity enhancements—supporting rigorous certification and verification processes. By recording every step in a secure, decentralized database, blockchain technology minimizes fraud and ensures that sustainability claims can be independently audited. This transparency not only strengthens certification schemes for regenerative agriculture but also increases confidence for buyers and investors who seek proof of environmental and social benefits.

Enhancing Market Access Through Verified Sustainable Sourcing:

Verified traceability is increasingly a prerequisite for accessing premium markets, including those demanding climate-smart, organic, or regenerative products. Blockchain-enabled systems track produce from farm to shelf, documenting its environmental footprint and compliance with sustainability standards. Producers using regenerative methods can command higher prices and secure long-term contracts with buyers seeking responsible sourcing. Retailers and brands, in turn, benefit from greater supply chain visibility, reduced risk, and enhanced reputation in sustainability-conscious markets.

Smart Contracts for Ecosystem Services Delivery:

Smart contracts—self-executing digital agreements coded on blockchain platforms—enable automated, transparent transactions tied to ecosystem service outcomes. For example, payments for carbon sequestration, biodiversity enhancement, or water retention can be released automatically when independent verification criteria are met and recorded on the ledger. This approach reduces transaction costs, ensures timely payments, and minimizes disputes, making it easier for farmers to participate in ecosystem markets and for funders to track impact. Smart contracts support innovative financing models, such as results-based payments and decentralized grants, further accelerating the adoption of regenerative practices.

By harnessing blockchain and traceability technologies, regenerative agriculture can demonstrate impact with greater credibility, access new revenue streams, and scale participation in value chains that reward environmental stewardship and climate action.

3.5 Innovation Ecosystems and Public-Private Collaboration

Scaling regenerative agriculture requires dynamic innovation ecosystems that bring together diverse stakeholders to develop, test, and disseminate effective solutions. Public-private collaboration accelerates knowledge transfer, fosters co-creation, and enables the rapid scaling of context-appropriate technologies and practices across farming systems.

Open-Source Platforms for Regenerative Knowledge Dissemination:

Open-source digital platforms are democratizing access to the latest knowledge on regenerative agriculture. These platforms aggregate and share research findings, practical guides, training materials, and data on soil health, biodiversity, and climate resilience. By making information freely available, open-source initiatives empower farmers, extension officers, policymakers, and entrepreneurs to adopt and adapt regenerative techniques suited to their local conditions. Interactive features, such as forums and decision-support tools, further enhance peer learning and facilitate the co-development of regionally relevant solutions.

Living Labs and Farmer-Led Innovation Networks:

Living labs and farmer-led innovation networks are powerful vehicles for participatory research, experimentation, and knowledge exchange. Living labs involve real-world settings where farmers, researchers, businesses, and community members collaborate to test regenerative practices, monitor outcomes, and refine techniques through iterative learning. Farmer-led networks drive bottom-up innovation, enabling producers to share experiences, troubleshoot challenges, and validate solutions on the ground. These approaches ensure that new technologies and practices are practical, scalable, and tailored to the realities of diverse farming landscapes.

Research-Industry Partnerships to Scale Context-Appropriate Technologies:

Strategic partnerships between research institutions, agri-tech companies, and public agencies are essential for advancing and scaling innovations in regenerative agriculture. Collaborative research programs accelerate the development of climate-smart seeds, biological inputs, digital monitoring tools, and mechanization tailored to local environments. Industry involvement brings technical expertise, manufacturing capacity, and pathways to market, while public support can de-risk investment and facilitate regulatory approval. By working together, research and industry partners can bridge the gap between laboratory breakthroughs and widespread adoption in the field, ensuring that regenerative technologies deliver tangible benefits for farmers, communities, and the environment.

A robust innovation ecosystem, grounded in collaboration and open knowledge exchange, is vital for mainstreaming regenerative agriculture and realizing its full potential to restore soils, enhance biodiversity, and strengthen rural economies worldwide.

Conclusion

Regenerative agriculture stands as a transformative solution for aligning global food production with the urgent imperatives of climate resilience, ecosystem restoration, and equitable rural development. By restoring soil health, enhancing biodiversity, and harnessing ecosystem services, regenerative systems generate benefits that reach far beyond increased yields—supporting water security, carbon sequestration, and sustainable livelihoods. As this Insight demonstrates, scaling regenerative agriculture requires coherent policy frameworks, innovative financing, and widespread adoption of digital and biological technologies, all grounded in inclusive, multi-level governance and international cooperation.

The way forward depends on collective action across government, financial institutions, the private sector, and farming communities. Policy coherence, targeted investment, robust monitoring, and cross-sector partnerships are essential for creating enabling environments where regenerative agriculture can thrive at scale. Innovation ecosystems, open knowledge sharing, and participatory approaches further ensure that solutions are locally adapted and widely adopted. As countries pursue net-zero and nature-positive goals, regenerative agriculture offers a practical, future-oriented foundation for resilient food systems and restored landscapes. With bold leadership and sustained collaboration, regenerative agriculture can become a cornerstone of climate-resilient development, restoring the world's soils and securing long-term planetary health for generations to come.

www.ingramcontent.com/pod-product-compliance
Lightning Source LLC
Chambersburg PA
CBHW060531280326
41933CB00014B/3140